if i ran the zoo

This place is too stuffy, too wild, or too calm.
Everything's all wrong and I know just the way to
make things right. It's time to stand up, to shake out
and roar. It's time to let loose and flap those wings.
It's time to swim upstream, to take a flying leap
to the next highest branch, to crow and strut and
bellow. It's time to buckle down, to hunker down,
to roll over and hibernate. In my zoo we move
freely, we eat what we like, we speak the languages
of all things that grow, hiss, and howl. I make my
own rules, I laugh and I play, I find my own way
because I run the zoo.

The most exciting phrase to hear in science, the one that heralds new discoveries, is not "Eureka!" ("I found it!") but "That's funny...."

—Isaac Asimov

The secret to life is to know when enough is enough.

—Dr. Vincent Ryan

Make it new.
   —Ezra Pound

People are always blaming their circumstances for what they are. I don't believe in circumstances. The people who get on in this world are the people who get up and look for the circumstances they want and if they can't find them, make them.

—George Bernard Shaw

*Your future depends
on many things, but
mostly on you.*

—Frank Tyger

There are many ways to victimize people. One way is to convince them that they are victims.

—Karen Hwang

*Choose thy love. Love
thy choice.*

    —German proverb

Play is the only way the highest intelligence of humankind can unfold.

—Joseph Chilton Pearce

*When you realize
how perfect everything
is you will tilt your
head back and laugh
at the sky.*

—Buddha

The pursuit of truth and beauty is a sphere of activity in which we are permitted to remain children all our lives.

—Albert Einstein

Small minds are concerned with the extraordinary, great minds with the ordinary.

—Blaise Pascal

*If the fool would persist
in his folly he would
become wise.*

—William Blake

Know your lines and don't bump into the furniture.

—Spencer Tracy

I have not failed. I've just found 10,000 ways that don't work.

—Thomas Edison

Life loves to be taken
by the lapel and told:
"I'm with you kid.
Let's go."

—Maya Angelou

I am pretty fearless, and you know why? Because I don't handle fear very well; I'm not a good terrified person.

—Stevie Nicks

To change one's life:
Start immediately, do
it flamboyantly, no
exceptions, no excuses.

—William James

The Constitution only gives people the right to pursue happiness. You have to catch it yourself.

—Benjamin Franklin

*We don't stop playing
because we turn old,
but turn old because
we stop playing.*

—George Bernard Shaw

_So long as you are still
worried about what
others think of you, you
are owned by them.
Only when you require
no approval from
outside yourself can you
own yourself._

—Neale Donald Walsch

When one man, for whatever reason, has the opportunity to lead an extraordinary life, he has no right to keep it to himself.

—Jacques Cousteau

Every strike brings me closer to the next home run.

—Babe Ruth

Another belief of mine:
that everyone else
my age is an adult,
whereas I am merely
in disguise.

—Margaret Atwood

*We cannot seek
achievement for ourselves
and forget about progress
and prosperity for our
community. . . . Our
ambitions must be broad
enough to include the
aspirations and needs of
others, for their sakes and
for our own.*

—César Chávez